For Maurice + Robb[illegible] August 2013

PEPPER GREASE

The Summer Season @ the Hollywood Bowl was made so much more enjoyable with you there

All the Best to you on Jews Name!

[illegible]

PEPPER GREASE

A Book of Poems for Those
with a Flavorful Soul

HARDY KEITH EDWARDS

iUniverse, Inc.
Bloomington

PEPPER GREASE
A Book of Poems for Those with a Flavorful Soul

iUniverse books may be ordered through booksellers or by contacting:

iUniverse
1663 Liberty Drive
Bloomington, IN 47403
www.iuniverse.com
1-800-Authors (1-800-288-4677)

ISBN: 978-1-4759-6221-5 (sc)
ISBN: 978-1-4759-6222-2 (ebk)

Printed in the United States of America

iUniverse rev. date: 2/16/2013

Contents

Part I

Mama's Son

Part II

Haiku & Senryu

Part III

The World and Me

Dedication

For My Mother Loretta Irene Eason
Whom I Love and Admire Profoundly

Foreword

Through Pain and Misery
Struggle and Strife
Adversity and Sorrow

There is Hope

Hope is the Key
Let it Unlock our Souls unto the Truth

Faith becomes the Beacon
that Guides our Way

God is Love

Acknowledgments

There are many I would like to thank for bringing
Pepper Grease to its publication.

First of all, I must acknowledge those individuals from
iUniverse whose professionalism and encouragement were
considerably significant in the development and completion
of this book: Rey Tome, Mars Alma, and Cherry Noel
respectively. My sincere appreciation goes to Joshua Flores,
Michelle Morgan, and Jeff Bristow for munificently aiding
me in many of the essential elements and organizational
components needed for the content dimensions of the
manuscript which I aspired. Their suggestions and assistance
were very significant in my work.

I'd like to thank my CSUN colleagues in the Schools
of the Arts & Humanities, the PAS Department's Writing
Program, Human Resources, and the great support from
those in the CSUN Michael D. Eisner School of Education,
most especially Dean Michael Spagna, Dr. Merril Simon,
and Dr. Greg Jackson, all of whom were instrumental in my
personal growth as an educator and a counselor. A treasured
legacy, a deeply revered sage for the ages, and an irrevocable
source of magnanimous achievement, Dr. Kayte M. Fearn,
believed in me when no one else would. May God Bless her
sweet marvelous soul everlasting. Thank you as well to the
wonderful health care providers who soundly remind me to
uphold healthy choices and wellness as keys to a good life:
Dr. Roger Quinney, Dr. Holly Kim, Dr. Haewon Choi, Dr.
David Alpan & Claudia *("Just Keep Smiling.")*, Dr. Victor
Beer, Dr. Steven Schenkle, Dr. Robert Baxley, Chidi Njoku,
and Madame Mayrce Boulange *("Reading is truly a joy
& the love of beauty is our eternal duty.")* Together, these
dedicated educators and medical practitioners have kept me
well and whole.

Most endearingly, I thank my truly blessed and wonderful family who have have always supported my noble endeavors, and they have steadily urged me to be humble and grateful for all things righteous and honorable. My cousin Mario Eason, one of my erudite companions, has been among those who have been very inspirational in my becoming a devoted author and poet.

My proven dear friends have shown me the values of joyful expression and creative verve; thank you to my most cherished of all Ms. Vanessa Lynn Townsell *("You better write or I'll pop you one good!")*; Roy "Daddy Ro" Navarro who insisted I stay focused on the positive (*"Always Keep Ya Head Up! Go Hard! & Make it Happen Big ED!"*); most vigorously, I offer a very special thank you to Gary Borden, my mentor & friend, and the most generously forceful guide I have known for actualizing the meritorious goals I have had in life. Thank you Coach Ed Stracher for Promoting Peaceful Prayers, Uplifting Our Reading Genius, and Illuminating Hearts & Minds World Wide. Finally, I enthusiastically thank Johnny Safi, Pepper Grease's book cover graphic designer and concept artist, whose creative collaboration was most instrumental in bringing the vision I had for the book to its fruition.

Thank You All! HKE "Big ED"

Preface

Letter to the Reader

Language is a vessel of immeasurable travels. May your journeys be as boundless and as wonderful as your hopes and dreams may carry you. Knowledge is power; our imagination is much more potent. There are no true certainties other than the constancy of change. Therefore, we must keep striving, keep believing, and keep evolving. May you have joy everlasting with the satisfying quest and promise of having the freedom to say what you mean and mean what you say.

As a direct descendant of Sojourner Truth, it has been part of my personal mission to keep the vibrancy of her legacy alive through both my daily deeds and the faithful practices of prayer for my people and for all of humanity. I ask that you uphold these values and virtues as well.

My hope is that you will enjoy and share this book as one reflective of the rich culture which is that of the African American experience. May we be continually reminded from whence we've come, so that we might boldly, creatively, skillfully, passionately, and resoundingly pursue a posterity of prosperity for ourselves, our communities, and our world; as we do so, may it be in the name of peace and all things beautiful, true, great, and good. May the light and love of our Lord be your sources of strength today and always.

Earnest Regards, H.K. Edwards

I

Mama's Son

Rhythm of the City

Rhythm of the City
       Makes the dog bark makes the bird sing
             Grandma wash the bathtub ring
Them greens cooking in the pot sho smell good
       Uncle ain't working but wish that he would

Find a job that pays more than 25 cent thrills
       'cause the bills
             keep comin' and they don't care
who they hurt who they scare
       They will jump over Liberty
           beat down on Freedom
               lie about Tomorrow
       and steal your dreams Today

Yeah Rhythm of the City
       keeps-on-a-beatin' a-ratta-tat-tat & stuff-like-that
for the rich man's dance or the poor man's song . . .
       the melodies of hope and what the good heart brings

Save the city children masked in illusion
       drugs and violence weaved in confusion

Change the beat to a Sweeter Chord
       Somebody do Something
           If not you Dear Lord

Just Us

Who dat down dere in da gutter
with the needle in dey veins . . .
Just us
Who dat in da prison cells
criminally insane . . .
Just us
Who be makin' all dat noise
in dem gangster limosines . . .
Just us
Who are the children whose lives
are bustin' at the seams . . .
Just us
Who be da homeless, da hongree
and da nominally deprived . . .
Just us
Who are the peoples dying from
AIDS in the prime of their lives . . .
Just us
Who can shine the American Constitution
and bring about a change?
Just us

What is the answer to the problem
some afraid to ponder?

Justice!

for

JUST US

Life

a bowl of sweat

a sad regret

a heap of debt

a momentary smile

a tested faith

a world of people

who do not care

Life

So Dang Hot!

Nope, I ain't got no fancy car
But my mind can go just as far

Nmm Nmm, I ain't got no fancy clothes
But I can grow a yellow rose

I ain't got no money to shine
But what I got is all mine:

A dream that lives
A promise of hope
A glistening vision
A heart that is warm

A young child's smile makes it all worthwhile
When feeling the lows of life's brutal blows

I keep on pushing 'til the day arrives
When money is no object, only our lives
Filled with music, good health
Love and bliss, a tender kiss . . .

So I ain't sorry for what I ain't got
'Cause what I got is So Dang Hot!

My Dictionary

I SIT BESIDE MY DICTIONARY
ITS WEALTH SO STRONG AND SURE

WORDS OF PEACE DYNAMIC CHANGE
AND CRIME'S FORGOTTEN CURE

DIVERSITY A FAVORITE RHYME
TO ADVERSITY'S BEST TOOL

IGNORANCE AND STUPIDITY
NO FAULT OF ANY SCHOOL

I SIT BESIDE MY DICTIONARY
AND READ THE WORDS IN PRINT

GLAD TO KNOW HOW RICH I AM
THOUGH I HAVEN'T GOT A CENT

Hollywood

I

If Hollywood could, it would, do what it should
to propagate more good

It's who you know or who you blow
and whose 'privates' you will show
that get you where you go

A casting couch or director's chair
A writer's whim or producer's dare

Egocentric maniacs
for power and control
sex begets the drugs
begets the winner of the role
nepotism, private lies, and racism that is old

II

But Hollywood knows its own
wretched duality narcissistic frivolity
it revels in the cursory arts
and prides itself too great
to glance into equality
or ever hesitate
to balance what is wrong with degenerated youth
who raised on Hollywood Today
can barely learn or ever come to say
'thank you' in the simplest way . . .

For need of greed
the evil seed
of Hollywood . . .
We Plead, Take Heed

Thought!

A Professor said to me . . .
Read and read again
Discover the virtues of scholarship
When choices mirror sin

Like Franklin, Benjamin once wrote
the ways to wealth and wisdom
come easily to the moral man
who is ethical but tiresome
from hard day's work and effort pure
and yet despite adversity
he knows that he shall endure

Let's take a voyage said he
let's try to get away
escape our social maladies
realize the things we say

We'll journey through experience
of authors henceforth past
we'll raise our minds to infinite
farther higher faster than fast
zoom beyond the zenith of imagination's womb
See into complexities of mystic leaders' tombs

Fear not what ails you, said he,
Cast worry and doubt aside
Surrender unto Enlightenment
Do without false pride

Fulfill potential temperament
Let nature run its course
Reflect upon diversity
Firmament and the stars, a horse

Dream about the yesterdays tomorrow shall never see
then walk or talk and smile awhile and think eternity

Shoe Fly

The summer day was hot and sticky and mean
So I goes to open the door screen
Say'd come on in Mr. Fly
I asks no questions why
You buzz 'round without an utter
Den lands on my dairy butter
Bothering me even when I say please
Spreading dem nasty germs and household disease

"But come on in Mr. Fly
I won't ask no questions why
your babies is born in maggot clusters
of filth and garbage, decay and waste . . .
or just about anything you can muster."

"So, do, come on in Mr. Fly
I won't ask no questions why
you do what you do with the dogshit outside
wit yo' luminescent eyes opened so damned wide
But you keep away from my children, ya' hear
'cause Sunday's newspaper on top-the-table is near
Oh, I don't want to hurt you Mr. Fly
but if I has to I will
when up against the wall
I might just kill!"

Pepper Grease

No one could cook quite like Mama
    "Must be all that pepper," I'd say
'Or maybe that 'ol grease you use'
Mama'd keep on cooking and smiling while she
    sweetly sang the blues
      "Baby how long since you seen ya Daddy?"
        she asked rather quietly
"I don't know," I said
    "I hear he ain't doin' too good
seems he had another nervous breakdown
and he ain't acting like he should
people on the corner tell me he's married again
some say he raped my sister, and that's just an
unforgivable sin, another told me he messed up my brother
made him sleep out in the rain, and that he tried to break his legs,
it's all just too much for me Mama, and I don't know what to do
I really am afraid to call, he might try to hurt me too
what if people been lying about the dirt they seen?"
    "You never know lessen you talk with him son
    No need for fear my dear
    Once you've tried, you've won," she'd say

But over and over I thought to myself
How can I keep this thing on the shelf?
Damn, I need to get it off my chest
How else in the world can I be my best?

    Mama kept on humming and moaning the blues

I munched down my dinner
    Thinking 'bout Daddy's green alligator suede shoes

A Somber Chance

The difference between Life & Death

is queer unrest

Life is a bitch

until you find your niche

Heaven and Hell and the Here and Now

Life is still a Mystery

cain't nobody tell you how

Ego Rap

I love myself that's why the girls love me
'cause all we ever talk about is our vanity

how much money you have and what you plan to spend
how fine you are is all that counts in the end

she's got Gucci underwear and Halston pantyhose
since drugs are out of style
there ain't nothin' up her nose

I'm the baddest and the best so forget about the rest
I'm a winner every time
(just don't put me to the test)

when you think about it baby, there ain't
nothin' more to say I'll be playah number one
till the dawn of our new day

yeah ~ so if you think you've got an ego
you better think again

'cause the winner of the race
is the One who doesn't sin

Lay My Burden

LAY MY BURDEN SWIFTLY
THE RUNNER OF MY SOUL
STARVE MY NEEDLED HUNGER
BEGUILE MY INNER GOAL

LAY MY BURDEN DROWNING
THE ANCHOR-PADDED SWIM
BUILD A TEAR-FILLED RESERVOIR
OF LAMPS THAT HAVE GONE DIM

LAY MY BURDEN CRAWLING
THE MERCY OF THE NAIL
HAMMER ALL MY NICETIES
IMPRISON ME IN JAIL

LAY MY BURDEN PLEADING
THE JUSTICE NOW UNKNOWN
WAIVER ALL MY FACULTIES
AND CRUSH MY BRITTLE BONES

LAY MY BURDEN DEFTLY
THE ASHES FROM THE FIRE
SILENCE ALL THE WRETCHED NOISE
MY ANGER DID INSPIRE

SOUNDFLAKES

DISTANT EYES THAT SEEM TO HEAR

THE SOUNDFLAKES WHEN NO ONE IS NEAR

A SOLITUDE OF GROUP DESIRES

TRANSLUCENT WONDERS DAYS INSPIRE

SPACE AND TIME WITHIN MY MIND ARE

AVENUES WHO ADVANCE UTOPIA

FLORAL IMAGES ON A RAINBOW SPRING

FALL OF DECEPTION SHADOWED BY A WHITER THING

THE TRUTH TO BE . . .

SOUNDFLAKES THAT COME TO ME

AS CAROUSEL DREAMS PONDER
LISTLESSLY THROUGH THE NIGHT

STARS TWINKLE FAR FROM SIGHT

WINNERS ARE WINNERS WHO FIGHT THE FIGHT

RESIST DAMNATION AND ABOMINATE OUR PLIGHT

SOUNDFLAKES KEEP COMING NEARER TO THE DAY

WHEN WE SHALL SEE THE PERFECT WAY

'88'

Eighty-Eight   Eventful Great
Life and Love
Death and Hate

It isn't easy to surmise
the promise beyond the disguise
the misfortune of the yet incurred
the revelation of the word

Trusting makes it easier
reality sets it clear
surge ahead in Faith and See
an even better year?

The troubles that confront us
political and such
when tried against humanity
just don't seem like very much

But in '88' it's funny
the illusion many aspire
to have without labor to heat without fire
status quo possessions materials of wealth
luxuries and fantasies inclusive with good health
a showy exhibition has become the new condition
a never ending pension for corruption and derision

Greedy theories ineptly prove
to be unrefined and unduly rude
lacking in the social graces of money's higher places
and yet cannot stand to see the land
polluted and abused like man

Think that's enough to stop the cycle
perpetual and obscene?
No, think me not, the need for greed
out-shines the meanest green

'88' will save us though, the idealist cries alone
too many hungry too many seeking
too many on their own
too many problems unresolved
beyond our human means
too many complications to ignore
or so this is as it may seem

All has not been lost some may say
Hope may even have been restored
'88' was really rather quite exciting
much too busy for us to be bored

Just Another Nigma
Huh Nigma?

What did you say? I can't understand you man...
What did you just do? That ain't ordinary!

Feeling the stigma
                    Just another nigma
Different from the rest
                    You strive to be the best
       But the quest leaves you no rest
       Even through some say you're blessed

You're a fool to believe as you do
       Every thing we know isn't true
Sometimes being an enigma
       Feels more like a stigma
So how you figure,
                    Huh nigma?

Truth Be Told

What's right is never wrong both all day or night long
Though some protest this claim irrefutable it remains

As quiet as it is kept Mother Mary for Jesus wept
Her tears bemoan the aching echoes of her cries
Some may assert she moaned most the stain of satan's lies
There is no life of which we know hereafter there is only death

Solemn remains of those who sustain unknown
Perils in pain or whatever else we disdain
Honesty has a tendency to illustrate propensities
Sinuously towards a trust in despondency

An axiomatic dramatic criterion equivocates it clear again
Another referential case of indifference conditional
Prismatically dimensional or one of an otherwise
Exceptionally ready steady thrust of our full potential

Request

WHEN I AM GONE AND RESTING AWAY

DON'T CRY FOR ME, HEAR WHAT I SAY

SPARE YOUR TEARS AND DO NOT WEEP

FOR I AM HAPPIEST WHILST I SLEEP

IN A LAND OF DREAMS AND PROMISES FULFILLED

WHERE BETTER TOMORROWS ARE FOREVER WILLED

THY WILL BE DONE, THY WILL IS TRUE

SO DO NOT MOURN MY FRIEND

THOUGH I WOULD YOU

Journey

You are what you are
        before you ever become
what you'll be

You've seen what you saw
        before you'll ever see
what you'll see

You can get what you want
        before you ever need
what you have

You have cried a thousand smiles
        before you sob a single laugh

You will hear what you heard
        before you ever heard what
you're hearing

You are far away from journey voyages
        before you ever know you are nearing

What is - is and has been
        shall become not listening;
feeling before ever more numb

The Ship of Asperation and Determination's Fleet
        Jolts a New Awareness to Once Unmoving Feet

ALPHA OMEGA

A   Accords the Alphabet, Apples, Animals, Apricots, Allah, Acrobat
      Appreciation, Abundance, Admiration, Aesthetics, Action, Ankh

B   is the Blessing of Beauty, Bumble Bees, Bahamian Breezes, Baby,
      Bears, Brahma, Being, Books, Bugs, Buildings, Basketball, Bolt

C   Candy, Cakes, Cookies, Ice Cream, California, Comets, Calculus
      Comedy, Chicago, Currency, Corn, Creativity, Columbia, Cocoa

D   Divinity, Deeds, Decisions, Division, Democracy, Dodecahedrons,
      Doctors, Dogs, Donations, Denmark, Dallas, Denzel, Dentists, Dates

E   Evolution, Education, Easter, Elephants, Ewoks, Egalitarianism,
      Etymology, Emu, Electrons, Existence, Equilibrium, Equator, Eggs

F   is Forever, Feelings, Freedom, Friendship, Flowers, Fun, Fulcrum, Figs
      Food, Fusion, Faith, Fish, Flight, Feet, Frontiers, Frogs, Feasts, Finances

G   The Glory of God, Goodness, Gregariousness, Grandfathers, Greenland,
      Grapes, Gallantry, Saint Gregory the Great, Groundling, Groups, Gurus

H   Heaven, Happiness, Hymns, Hiroshima, Hippopotamus, Homage, Hemp,
      Heraldry, Humor, Hieroglyphics, Hercules, Hanukkah, Heuristics, Hawaii

I   Ideas, Identity, Ivory, Intelligence, Invention, Inquiry, Illumination,
      Image, Ibis, Israel, Ignitions, Impressions, India, Iron, Isthmus, Italy

J   Jesus, Jews, Jubilant, Jumping Joy, Jehovah, Jazz in Japan, Judo, Jacks,
      Jamaica, Juice, Jitterbug, Jacaranda Tree, Jewelry, Jobs, June Bugs, Jah

K   Kindness, Kangaroos, Karate, Karma, Keys to the Kingdom, Kyushu,
      Kung Fu, Krishna, Kabuki, Kentucky, Knuckles, Korea, Kim Chee, Kudos

L   Love, Laughter, Life Everlasting, Ladder, Laboratories, Libraries, Lyrics
     Lilacs, Learning, La Crosse, Labyrinths, Leaders, Lions, Lyceum, Land

M   Movies, Music, Money, Medicine, Mothers, Modern Media, Memories,
     Miracles, Macaroni, Mountains, Magnetism, Manners, Metamorphosis

N   Nature, Native Americans, Neighbors, Nepal, Neutrons, Nickels, Now
     Nighttime, Nourishment, Nashville, Nuts, Numerology, Negroes, Neon

O   is Ocean, Openings, Ovations at the Oscars, Olives, Otters, Omnipotence,
     Oaths, Objects, Okapi, Officials, Orlando, Oasis, Orbits, Oregon, Outfits

P   Pride, Peace, Power, Prayer, Panama, Philadelphia, Protons, Paraguay,
     Pagoda, Psychology, Paleontology, Pampero, Percussion, Peru, Pilgrims

Q   Quintessence, Quiddity, Quilts, Quadratic Equations, Quarks, Queue
     Quests, Quantity, Quorum, Quotations, California Quails, Quartz, Quasar

R   Rest, Relaxation, Redemption, Reality, Reason, Roosters, Rice, Rain,
     Recollections, Representation, Rivers, Rook, Ryukyu Islands, Rapture

S   Sheep, Soap, Sharing, Salvation, Sensibility, Soup, Shalom, Snowfall
     Saffron, Security, Seville, Selma, Sunshine, Sidewalks, Sierra Nevada

T   Theater, Truth, Talent, Teachers, Time, Thistles, Taiwan, Teeth, Tomatoes
     Tables, Taxonomy, Turkey, Tortoises, Tumbleweeds, Treats, Town, Tibet

U   is Ultraviolet, Unique, Uranography, Utopia, Ultimate, Uranus, Usher
     Upolu, Underground Railroad, UFOs, Ukulele, Ulna, Ukraine, Uranium

V   View, Valor, Velocity, Vietnam, Vote, Vegetables, Vitamins, Vacation, Volt,
     Volume, Vatican City, Volunteers, Vigilance, Virginia, Volcanoes, Vroom

W   is the Wiz, Water, Women, Words, Wine, Work, Waves, Washington D.C,
Winners, West Hollywood, Wheels, Whirlwind, Wonk, Wunderkind

X   Xylophones, Xerxes, Xenon, X-Rays, Xenia, Xylography, Xingu, Xhosa,
Xerophyte, Xylem, eXcellent, eXciting, eXceptional, eXhilarating lives (!)

Y   is Yahweh, Yams, Yesterday, Yosemite, Youth, Yoga, Yak, Yuletide Carols,
Yonder, Yellowstone, Yield, Yucca, Y-Chromosome, Yearbook, Yearning

Z   Our Zimbabwe, the Zoo, Zygote, Zymosis, Zebras, Zoroastrianism, Zippers
Zululand, Zebu, Zilch, Zen Philosophy, and our Zany Zenith Zodiac ways

Myriads of Mystical Meanings
Astounding Never-Ending
Symphonic Reckoning
Our Evolutionary Destiny

Alpha Omega

For the Graduate

Congratulations! My erudite companion

Your institutional recognition
    is the epitome of future success

You are the one who will make the rhetoric of
        Peace a more desirable mode

What will you do now with the Truth
        You have gained

Cure our social ailments
            or perpetuate the pain

I Know You Will Choose What Is Right

Just as law is at times a swiftly changing thing
    it truly doesn't matter what or which song you sing

For the graduate
    the world becomes a
        habitable habitual domain

Dreams As They Seem

I DREAMED ONE DAY THAT I HAD TOUCHED A VISION
I SAW HER THERE, SO UNAWARE, EVEN AS I TOUCHED HER HAIR

SHE MOVED WITH CHARM, WITH STYLE AND GRACE,
SHE MOVED AS SMOOTHLY AS A CAT TO EACH AND EVERY PLACE

I SANG A SONG FOR HER SWEET AND BEAUTIFUL SOUL
SHE LISTENED VERY CAREFULLY AND CLOSED HER EYES TO SEE
SHE SAW A FLEETING DEER, AND FIELDS OF BLOOMING DAISIES
SHE SAW THE SUNLIGHT'S ARMS REACH OUT
TO TOUCH THE SUBTLE DAWN

THEN I SAW HER WALK INTO THE VALLEY GRAND

THEN I SAW THE SWEET AND PEACEFUL VALLEY
THAT SHE LOOKED UPON

THE PURPLE AND THE AMBER HILLS WITH
PINK SHADED CLOUDS ABOVE

SHE GAZED ABOUT THE NEAR GREEN PASTURES
WITH EYES MADE OF LOVE

SHE DISAPPEARED INTO DARKNESS
AND I FELT MYSELF WAKE UP

THEN I REALIZED THAT I HAD SPENT A DREAM WITH GOD

AND AN ANGEL HAD TOUCHED MY HAND

Whimsical, My Amorous Whim

What is this Whimsical?
Am I Whimsical?
Bizzare or just mundane

For why I should fantasize, seek,
and then obtain
the common superficialities
that cause the temporate bequethed rains
Assunder and cast derisions
darkened utterance and swear
scorn the late-in-blooming

and question the play-indulgent-game
Moderation aside
Miraculous recovery

Second-chance for the have-on-with-in
who've forgotten to ponder
conditional adaptation
and reflect again . . .

So why am I so whimsical?
Things ordinary and plain
just don't spark the change

Dash! My fight's intensified
A Rebel of Today - Sublime
Shielded Commonplace

Flash! Whimsical Deeds
My Love in Mind

BODY DANCE

Body Dance
Body Dance Let Memory Go
Feel a Cosmic Constant Flow
The Rhythms of the Oceanwide

Crystal Sands Where Blue Stones Reveal Paradise
Waves of Love Kiss the Shore ~ Once and Never More

Where No Man Can Go with Spirit Bound
This Place of Beauty Where Colors Are Found
Colors of All in One ~ One in All Colors

Body Dance Let Memory Go
Dance for Joy Feel Percussion Grow
Ride the Wave of Desire Healing Beating of the Drum
Taste the Fruit of Passion ~ Feel Percussion Grow

Asia Africa America Universal Awareness
Amazing How Different Yet One the Same
Desultory Desperate Despair ~ Who's to Blame?

We Search for Answers on the Street
Our Bodies Dancing Our Moving Feet
Unchained Uplifted Free Spirited Fly
Curiously Irresolutely We ~ Wonder How or Why

Body Dance Let Memory Go
Feel a Cosmic Constant Flow
The Rhythms of the Oceanwide

Cosmic Celebration

SOMETHING GREAT IS HAPPENING
YOU CAN SEE IT EVERYWHERE
PEOPLE CHANGING VALUES PROVING THAT THEY CARE

THE HEAVENS CRIED OUT LAST SPRING
FREELY POURING OUT ON EVERYTHING
RAINDROPS FALLING AND HURRICANES WAILING
MUDSLIDES AND FLOODS WE HAD TO STAND
ALL THROUGHOUT OUR GREATER GLOBAL LANDS

THE SKY IS INFINITE
IMAGINATION TOO
TIME FOR A COSMIC CELEBRATION
UNITED TOGETHER AS PANTHEISTS DO
CHRISTIAN MUSLIM BUDDIST JEW & HINDU TOO

HOLD TIGHT AND DON'T LET GO
ANOTHER WONDROUS WHIZZING SOLAR SHOW
SUPERNOVA COMETS IN THE SKY
SOJOURNER TRUTH RIDING HIGH

Angel Speak

MAGNIFICENT MOON
CELESTIAL STARS
BAHAMIAN BREEZES
ENGINELESS CARS

THANK YOU HEAVENLY FATHER
FOR ALL THAT YOU DO
YOU SHOW ME THE LIGHT
AND THE WAY AND THE TRUTH

I AM CHANGING MY HEART FOR YOU
BY GIVING A LOVE THAT'S INFINITELY NEW
NO MORE FALSE SET OF LIES
SUBJECT TO THE WEAKNESS OF MAN
BUT LIVING TO DO ALL THAT I CAN
THAT IS IN YOUR HANDS

IN KNOWING YOU I AM STRONGER AND I AM BRAVER
FREE FROM THE DAYS I KNEW AS A SLAVE
GONE IS THE WEARY MIND
THAT ONCE RULED ME UNABLE
NOW I SPEAK OF MERCY AND GRACE
LOVE AND REST IN GOD'S CRADLE

Tribute To Minnie Riperton

I HAD A BEAUTIFUL DREAM, I DREAMT
THAT I HAD MET YOU MINNIE

THERE YOU WERE IN MY DREAM
AND ALL I COULD THINK OF WAS PERFECTION

THERE WAS A WONDERFUL SLICE OF HEAVEN IN YOUR EYES
I STARED NOT WANTING TO PASS UP
THE OPPORTUNITY
THAT I WAS VIEWING A PERFECT ANGEL

YOU SMILED AND SAID HELLO TO ME.
THEN AT THAT CONCISE MOMENT,
I FELT A SURGE OF WARMTH,
AN UNCOMPLICATED LOVE
FOR A PERFECT ANGEL
AND A FEELING THAT WAS
DEEP AND MYSTICAL

Grateful ORINOZ

I smiled one day and made a wish
    That star I'd seen was bright
It helped me to see what was right
    I learned the parable of loaves and fish
Ever grateful of ORINOZ, overflowing cup on life's dish

I found that humans have come a long way
    Low points have made me feel dumb
Grateful ORINOZ has pointed out the high points to come
    Self-sacrifice is silly, I wanna stay
'Cause the great reward of hard work is play

He taught me Namaste' and to say, "We are One!"
    I recognize the light of God that shines in you
As I'm sure you recognize the light of God in me too
    The closeness of Family to Friends, play to fun
The growth of all things under the Sun

Grateful ORINOZ more and more each day
    Say Forever we'll stay this way
Visions Grand and marvelously preserved
    The good that comes your way is greatly deserved

Love, Life and Flowers, Clouds and Dreams
      Bees that buzz, Eagles that fly their own heights
            Martin Luther King and Civil Rights
Music that moves the Soul
            Knowledge that grooves the Mind
We are leaving the negative way behind

Grateful ORINOZ for the Mirror
      That showed me myself clearer
Growing and changing in every way
This is what I learned today
      Laughter and Joy, Man from Boy,
               Thank You

Anachronistic Love

When did I notice that smile so true?
     When did I notice that the sky is blue?
What was the reason for living to give?
     How do I explain that giving is to live?

Anachronistic; out of place stored in mind

It is True Love is Good,
     Do unto others as you would . . .
Have them do unto you?
     No, I don't think so
Just be good to satisfy yourself
     Not expectations, not secrets foretold
Just memories to keep and Dreams to Hold

Anachronistic; out of place on a misplaced shelf

Watch out dear children, be careful to hear
     Love is the answer, not lies and fear
So find your trusting love always to keep
     and plant the seed that only grows deep

Anachronistic; out of place, wrong time

PAPA IS A TREE

My father once was a strong black man
deep earthy muscular
a high school football player
All American USC
When he got his scholarship to the university
He turned it down, gave it up, he was just nineteen
and I was 8 pounds 10 ounces
He risked a rat-race responsibility, head-strong notions
over chance, promise, or future opportunity . . .

And then weakened by a furious fog
and some certain social vices
He tripped up on an ill-fated manner, one brashly divisive
He liked to fight He lost his job
then ate some devil-dope, and in so doing
He found a loss of faith and darkly degraded hopes

And ever since those dreadful nights
He had lived a life of wretched scornful hate

He slapped my mother's face
(occasion nebulously unsound)
or maybe even cocked her in the jaw
and in so doing spurred her love away
He let life's wicked forces
decisively tear our family apart

"He's crazy," people would tell me, too often it had been said
yet they offered not one worthy word comfort or cure
for his tortured troubled head
He wandered the streets like a vagabond all around town
or so I've been told
Displaced by social norms and crushed by tainted pasts
He alone consumed my constant clouds of doubts
and in so doing hurtfully tormented my hidden inner storms

When I think I might become what potential says I may
I battle with the thoughts or things that try to keep me down
with earnest hopes for seeing bigger better brighter days
some way some day some how

Solemn Surrender

I give thee unto Dreams

        unto itself manifest

in seams besewn

                by conquest

I alone Surrender

Empty Page

EMPTY PAGE YOU ARE A FRIEND

YOU LET ME BE AS I AM

I NEED NOT EVEN THINK TO PLEASE YOU

YOU SWEETLY RECEIVE ME HOWEVER I MAY BE

MELANCHOLY IN POVERTY OR JUBILANT IN ECSTASY

YOU NEVER LOOK AT ME WITH DESPICABLE SCORN

YOU SHOW YOU LIKE ME BECAUSE WE ARE EACH OTHER

I CAN FILL YOU UP, SCRATCH YOU, OR COCKLE-DOODLE YOU

AND YOU LET ME

I CAN BE OUTRAGEOUS OR GENTLE,
VORACIOUS OR CORDIAL
SULTRY OR SOPHISTICATED, INTELLIGENT OR DUMB
MEAN OR MAD

I LOVE YOU EMPTY PAGE

YOU KEEP MY THOUGHTS ALIVE

SAY I AM FOREVER YOURS

BECAUSE EMPTY PAGE YOU ARE HELL AND NIRVANA

THE SMILES I'VE KNOWN AND THE TEARS I'VE CRIED

YOU ARE TRUTH'S SOLDIER WHEN WARRIORS HAVE LIED

7 Things

parking pass, car keys,

ink pen, cell phone,

business card, sunglasses

soda pop on ice

Coffee

Dark   Rich

Strong   Black

Aromatic

and one more fact

recent medical and scientific studies have

also proven that in the right amounts

coffee

can be good for you too

Now put that in ya cup and drank it

Add cream and sugar if that's also what you like to do

Make It Funky Now

Is that the smell from my arm pits
or the stank from my drawers

    Is it the stench in the air
    or is that nasty nasty all yours

Is it the music in my soul
that keeps me well and whole

    Is it just that you ain't did nuthin' yet
    'cause you 'fraid to speak or break a sweat

Gossip and lies and false tales you reveal
You must be second cousin to that ugly fool the devil

    Beelzebub is it or maybe the Boogie Man in you
    Funky is as funky do, erebahdy know dats true

Get clean, stay lean, that's what they say
Get up, stay up, that's how the real funky play

    When the shit hits the fan or folk get in your way
    Just make it funky now, and you'll have a better day

Oh, tomorrow will be brighter   F-U-N-K
Y'all keep it funky . . .   Believe it!   Hey! Hey! Hey!

Invisible Touch

Hot Honesty
Hour of Danger
Day of Freedom
Odor of Joy
Sounds of Static

Feel   Clear   Visions

Peace   Harmony   Today

Cosmic Creator
Melodic Music
Universal Awareness
Jazz Alive
Spirit Thrive

Peace   Harmony

Today

II

Haiku & Senryu

A **Haiku or Senryu** is a Japanese style of poetry in a traditional three-line format or poetic structure of 17 syllables (5-7-5). So, what is the difference between Haiku and Senryu?

To some degree it doesn't matter because these labels are the tools of academic analysis, not poetic appreciation. Nevertheless, for analytic purposes ~ most poems that are Haiku or Senryu fall into four categories:

1) serious nature poems
2) serious human-centered poems
3) humorous nature poems (rare)
4) humorous human-centered poems

Senryu
Courage

Life for us is hard
Why so pusillanimous
Just to be is strength

Haiku
Flowers

Whilst picking flowers
Blooming in the morning sun
I remember you

Senryu
Wisdom

Know when to say when
If not then begin again
Just trust in yourself

Haiku
Wind

Warm the wind blows free
Enticing me to be true
Constant is its change

Senryu
Mother

She stands at the door
Quiet am I when she speaks
These words are not mine

Senryu
Father

Absent for so long
I wonder why this has been
He is not my friend

Haiku
Doubt

Not sure why it is
Creation mysterious
Originator

II
Uncertain it is
Creation a mystery
An original

Senryu
Brain

Profoundly robust
Magnificently sublime
God is within us

II
Thoughts of loveliness
Invention's progress drives us
Sweet yet cruel behold

Senryu
Gifts Beguiled

Pain and sadness mine
Some say I'm an angry man
Who can see my gifts?

Senryu
Celebrate the Date

Black History Month
Reflections upon our past
Tomorrow has come

Haiku
Alley Shade

Blossoms of clover
Yellow blooms on the pathway
It could be good luck

Senryu
Watchful Walk

You must be careful
Pace yourself be vigilant
Prepare for the best

Senryu
Rhythm of Life

Listen to its sound
My heart beats in my ear drum
Is that what I hear?

Haiku
Faded Beauty

Dead and dried flowers
Upon my cabinet they sit
Reminders of life

Haiku
Plant Life

Photosynthesis
Till the earth and plant the seeds
Joy shall nourish you

Senryu
Jumoke

Great among men
Courageous wise beautiful
God loves his true heart

Senryu
Lovely Gardenia

Lady sings the blues
Her songs sweeter than honey
Billie Holiday

Haiku
African Daisy

Purple etched bronze
Beauty is everlasting
Goddess of the sun

Haiku
Geranium

A geranium
Like a soft fan in my hand
The color is bright

Haiku
Two Birds

Up flies the seagull
A crow lands on a tree branch
Black and white in flight

Haiku
Rosemary

Sweet the aroma
Tiny branches stretch outward
Small purple orchids

Haiku
Heaven's Light

A purple sky
View our luminous expanse
Bright only at night

Haiku
Sky

Blue majestic vast
Shades the trees which branch above
Infinitely new

Senryu
Stop Ahead

Today I look forward
Unlike my doubts yesterday
So embrace my joy

Senryu
Inevitable Review

Cries of Columbine
Remember what happened there
How can we stop it?

Senryu
Macho Fears

Real men do not cry
Show not yourself with eyes full
Tears make you look weak

Senryu
Hold My Hand

None better to touch
Firm and sure I feel your grasp
Why do you let go

Senryu
Wonder

Imagination
The greatest gift we posses
Now think of nothing

Senryu
Soliloquist

Talking to myself
Others may know what I say
Do they understand

Haiku
Untamed Roses

Living ancestors
Dwell amongst fields plains mountains
Too many to count

Haiku
Bouquet

Pink red violet
Blooms the flowers of springtime
Gift of florescence

Haiku
The Fallen Leaves

I watch the leaves fall
Feel the gentle breeze
Knowing that God is

Senryu
Bag Man

The man with the bag
Looks down to see it swaying
Its contents unknown

Haiku
The Ants

Ants love the sweetness
The iris blossoms entice
Open eyes to see

Senryu
Arbitrary Boundaries

Streets full of fences
Keeping others out or in
Falsely makes home safe

Senryu
Laughing Whispers

Giggles and chuckles
Sometimes are not what they seem
So why do I laugh

Haiku
Gray the Day

Cloudy overcast
Sunshine hidden from our sight
Promises to keep

Senryu
Brown Shoes Unfound

I lost my brown shoes
Could not find them anywhere
Black ones do not fit

Senryu
TEACHER THREAT

You have no idea
What I'm gonna do to you
She said out of bounds

Senryu
IMF

You know what I mean
Insincere mother f*ckers
They care not for us

Senryu
Doldrums

Inactivity
When the going gets too tough
Anger becomes rage

Senryu
Sports Fan

Championship title
Does it get any better
Back to back it does

Senryu
Profundity

Say your prayers first
Make them something meaningful
Believe it is true

Senryu
Rear View

Out of the windows
Doorways to success are clear
Twenty twenty sight

Senryu
AIDS

Answers in deep science
Theoretical nonsense
We need a cure now

Senryu
Cooperation

Simple is as such
Do what one asks in kindness
There will be no mess

Senryu
Holy Sabbath

Remember to Rest
Keep the Sabbath Holy
Pray for Peace with God

Senryu
Temptations

Marvelous troubles
Tread lightly or risk your fate
All of us have them

Haiku
Wonderful Ignorance

An eagle in air
The way a snake slithers
Crests of ocean waves

Haiku
Butterflies

Chrysalis cocoons
Caterpillars eating leaves
Born to fly free

Haiku
Chimpanzee

Monkey sees a man
Wonders if we are cousins
Why are we so mean

Haiku
The Sea

Is it blue or green
Maybe it is in between
Does it not matter

Haiku
Spring Time

Trees green once again
Fully outstretched leaves will sprout
Giving us new life

Senryu
Blue Roses

Glass Menageries
Tennessee Williams once wrote
Some memories cost

Senryu
The Visit

May I see you soon
As illusive as time is
Please promise we shall

Senryu
Deadline

Silence the critic
Just do what must be done now
That is the best way

Senryu
Free Masons

Secret rituals
Only for the select few
Who built this nation

Senryu
Unemployed

Look for a new job
When they try not to see you
God knows what is right

Senryu
Uprising

Los Angeles fires
Watts in 1965
Fifty years later

Senryu
Honorary Privileges

Celebrate yourself
Just because you deserve it
Nobody like you

Senryu
Foolish Smoker

Spark it puff inhale
What are you doing to your lungs
You should know better

Senryu
Hubris

Weep original sin
Cite biblical prophecies
Haughty naughtiness

Senryu
The Squeeze

Where is the money
Decreasing income resources
Tightening our belts

Senryu
Sunday Service

Hear our pastor preach
Listen as the choir sings
Communion prayers

Senryu
Dye Log

When we conversate
Tell me that you understand
You Noah Eye Mean

Senryu
Pizza Pikachu

Delivery boy
Gave my grandmother free food
Devoted father good friend

Senryu
44

Barak Obama
United States President
First Lady Michelle

Senryu
Caesar Salad

Garlic bread croutons
Parmesan cheese vinaigrette
Oh so delicious

Senryu
Civil Service

One declaration
Iambic pentameter
Complications

Senryu
Lady Blue

Beautiful dark skin
Hip Hop Boosters President
Stop pulling my hair

Senryu
EINSTEIN

Relativity
Thermodynamics Theory
Kindness, Beauty, Truth

Senryu
Navigation Compass

Learn to read the stars
Your direction will be clear
Where are you going

Senryu
Radiance

Light overcomes shadows
Illuminating your mind
Genius in us all

Senryu
Common Thief

Robs you of your sleep
Takes away your favorite things
Better lock your doors

Senryu
May Day

Dance around maypoles
Workers protest union rights
Save our souls today

Senryu
Illusion

Promulgated fears
False evidence appearing real
Purgatory hell

Senryu
Halls of Injustice

Respect our children
Stop telling those awful lies
Karma will get you

Senryu
Tidings of Joy

Christmas ornaments
This year we have a real tree
Cheerful egg nog toasts

Senryu
Insomnia

Try to go to sleep
Close your eyes then rest your head
Long yawns alarm clocks

Senryu
Synchronicity

Working together
Unified theory constructs
All at the same time

Senryu
Whatever

Anyway you want
Makes no difference to me
Be spontaneous

Haiku
HKE

Helen Keller Eyes
See beyond knowing sight
Nature triumphant

Senryu
Convenient Amnesia

Man in the Mirror
Michael Jackson's favorite song
Illogical proof

Senryu
Acappella Candle

One Moment in Time
God Bless Miss Whitney Houston
Star Spangled Banner

Senryu
TAMU

Sweet Essence Pure Joy
Summer Class of 1960
Burgundy Mustang

Senryu
Double Struggle

Determination
Another problem to fix
Here we go again

Senryu
Cool Pockets

Keys coins jingling
Curiously bulging out
Is that what that is

Senryu
Dullards

Mannequin people
Is it not interesting
Boring happiness

Senryu
Roman Remains

USA Today
A mission of perdition
Unscrupulous quests

Senryu
Shallow

Wading in the pool
Considering going deep
Head first feet follow

Senryu
Pimple

Another face bump
Rising on my cheek again
Why on picture day

Senryu
Maybe

Perhaps luck finds us
Superficial tendencies
Might keep us apart

Senryu
Hunger

Thirsty for water
Chocolate ice cream sandwich
Restful sleep beckons

Senryu
Crystallization

Conquest Manifest
As One Thinks It Shall Be So
Possibilities

Senryu
Ascension

Jesus Christ Our Lord
Good Friday Sunday Service
We Are Forgiven

Senryu
Dear Katie Marie

Earn Your Turn Said Fearn
Diagramming Sentences
PRH Fellows

Senryu
Una Vez Por Favor

Tu Como La Flor
Selena Quintanilla
Gracias Amor

Senryu
Granchie Betty Boop

Say Goodnight My Love
Remember to Say Your Prayers
Family Comes First

Haiku
JAMBO!

Zikomo Yahya
Madzimoyo Azibo
Chionesu Zahur

Senryu
Queen Rosentine

None More Taskmaster
Afro-centric Legacies
Endearing Mentor

Senryu
Big Booty Trudy

See that sexy ass
The radio says smack it
That's what I shall do

Senryu
Sexified Saturday Nights

Carnal incarnate
Lascivious intentions
How good does it feel

Senryu
Homeostasis

Feel good vibrations
Chakra equilibrium
Spinal alignment

Senryu
Coordinates

Where are we headed
Lakes of fire unless we pray
Look for your heart first

Senryu
Nocturnal Submission

Sweet dreams dearest heart
One whom most would say admire
May we never part

Senryu
Godmother

I am Jan of Sam
Cummings Daune Thomas Bruce Don
Pee Wee Loves Reyna

Senryu
Fashion Funeral

Lugubrious shouts
Long sad obituary
Coffin matches shoes

Senryu
Isabella Born Free

Peter Sophia
Pa Dorothy Aunt Maxine
Live Long Love Irene

Senryu
Figueroa Street
(City of the Angels)

Los Angeles Pop
Hot Be Bop Jazz Razzmatazz
Central Avenue

Senryu
Cinco de Mayo
5*5*5

It is well alive
Another proclamation
Who says we are free

Senryu
Mismanagement

L A U S D
What a mess it has become
Cheating liars crooks

Senryu
Second Secant

Trigonometry
Ratio hypotenuse
Sine angle cosine

Senryu
Totem Pole

Hierarchical
Painted poles erect upright
Loyal subclass

Senryu
Encumbrances

Rude disallowances
Procrastination hindrances
Query suspicious

Senryu
Terminated

Final Agreement
Expropriated falsely
Dark lies negate truth

Senryu
High Rollers

Wheels turn while skates glide
Finger folded berry blunt
Gamble win or lose

Senryu
Spectator

Go people watching
Some love doing it daily
Different yet same

Senryu
SAD AVERAGES

Mediocrity
Enemy of our people
Why not be your best

Senryu
Mars Landing

Communications
Planetary voyages
Mission outer space

Senryu
Optimist

Look on the bright side
You know it could be worse
All is not so bad

Senryu
Pessimist

No one understands
What is the point of living
Another victim

Senryu
ENVY

Misanthropic deeds
Far from one gregarious
You want what I need

Senryu
PNP

Dens of inequity
Pathetic needless planning
Step boldly away

Senryu
LIQUOR

Raise your glass smile toast
Celebrate ceremonies
Please do not get drunk

Senryu
SIR PRIZE

Unexpected joy
Frivolity merriment
Thanks to you we laugh

Senryu
One Song

Universal gifts
Our most cherished talents be
Mind body heart soul

Senryu
GABRIEL

Believer of Christ
Always a wonderful man
You should know him too

Senryu
NEW MEXICO

Cool Buddy Kyle
Native American Smiles
Cascades of Red Rock

Haiku
Sycamore

John Steinbeck Once Wrote
Perfectibility Man
Something We Aspire

Senryu
Solamente' Tu Mi Amor

Jubilant feelings
I have those for you always
So I say today

Senryu
Caliente'

Hottest lava lust
So tasty upon my tongue
Commanding cold showers

Senryu
PROTECTION

Secure belongings
An indemnification
Who needs insurance

Senryu
MAMA SAID

Do your chores right now
If you want to play outside
Pay day allowance

Senryu
SOS

Stuck on Stupid
Problem Instigators
Save Our Souls Please God

Senryu
PALETTE

So many colors
Why is my gray outlook such
Paint a new picture

Haiku
Feathers of the Finch

Small songbirds short beaks
Gold cardinal canary
Seed eating sparrows

Haiku
Bougainvillea

Paradise Island
Colors of the Bahamas
Makes Me Think of Home

Haiku
SEQUOIA

California Trees
Oldest Growing Roots On Earth
Mighty Big Strong Tall

Senryu
EAGLE

Fairness flies most high
Egalitarian fact
Americans win

Senryu
Victory Ceremony

GOLDEN MEDALISTS
Olympic Games XXX
Historical Feats

Senryu
Flying Squirrel

Gabrielle Douglas
Our Magnificent Gymnast
Inspirational

Haiku
LUNA

Full Moon Rising East
Jupiter Mercury Mars
Syzygy Night Lights

Haiku
Eucalyptus

Cute Koala Bears
Native to Australia
Go Down Under Mate

Haiku
Hyssop

Fragrant blue flowered
Folk healing medicine plant
Sprinkling ancient rites

Haiku
IVY

Dionysus climbs
Grapes clings vines unconsciously
Bacchus red wine drink

Haiku
Horizon

Sand waves ocean sky
Beach pelicans seashells seals
What lies beyond these

III

The World and Me

Beckoning

I am what I am for reasons

unbeknownst to me

Therefore I am what I am

to be

Born Free

Brilliance

The senses tell what will be
      We are living miracles webbed in destiny
We who dream are truly free
      Bound in Hope and Promised though Faith

A zest for life as we live each day
      Peace for All this we Pray

Winter to Spring, Summer and Autumn too!
Visions of the Creator expressed for me and you

      When flowers bloom we always know
            that Life is Beauty, Love will Grow

      The Change of Seasons The Many Reasons

Namaste' We are One United by the Sun
      No Need for Fright We See the Light
      So Hear the Truth and Taste the Right

REFLECTIONS

STEP . . . A POOL OF WATER
    A VISION, A REFLECTION YOU THINK YOU SEE

STOP . . . A MIRROR
    A VISION OF A REFLECTION YOU THINK YOU SEE

PASS . . . THROUGH A GLASS
    A VISION IMPAIRED, NOT THAT OF A MIRROR
        UNSURPASSED

SIGHT . . . A VISION,
    NEAR REFLECTIONS, YOU THINK, YOU SEE

MOVEMENT . . . OUR WAY OF GETTING AROUND TODAY

REFLECTIONS HERE, REFLECTIONS THERE,
    HIGHER AND HIGHER, REFLECTIONS EVERYWHERE

BLACK, WHITE, BOTH A REFLECTION THROUGH MIND AND SIGHT

WHAT IS GREEN IS MINE, WHAT IS BLUE IS YOURS
    REFLECTIONS LIKE KEYS CAN OPEN DOORS

PEOPLE THE SAME IN ACTIONS
    BUT DIFFER TO SOCIETY BECAUSE OF SKIN DISTRACTION

REFLECTIONS, A WAY TO SEE
    WHEN INCORRECT SHOULD BE
        CORRECTED BY YOU AND ME

REFLECTIONS, REFLECTIONS,
    REFLECTIONS, REFLECTIONS
        REFLECTIONS . . .

GYRE

PYRAMIDAL ASCENSION
RISETH THE PHOENIX
DUST DAZZLED ASH

CRIMSON FLAME AFIRE
ENLIGHTENMENT REBORN
THROUGH OUR SHARED DESTINY HIGHER

PLANE NUANCE PLATEAU
ASKANCE FREQUENCY

COVERT OPERATIONS
ENTANGLED HOPS
JANGLED BOPS

JUST BE COOL
REMEMBER THE GOLDEN RULE
WHAT GOES AROUND COMES AROUND
KARMA DOGMA DHARMA

FEEL THE FIRE AS WE ASPIRE
THE RHYTHMIC PYRE OF THE GYRE

Lexophilia

love for words can become

a living breath to warm

even the coldest heart

so it seems when one

is so wrought with pain

or so sadly sewn to joy

ambivalent with the omnipotence

of the unyielding

inevitable truths of fate

circling cycles around the sun just for fun

destiny plays its hand

Death, 'tis Sweetest
Yet Unknown

Oh 'tis sweet to think of death as
quiet celebration
void of Life's complexities
simple joys unknown

When I think of twisted men
and women of foul intent
who rule our world's direction
I savor thoughts of emptiness
of death's indifferent contempt

Why fear the unsolved mystery?
As it is with Life so it is with Death

Death, it's magnetic charm is sure
lacking the modern deliberations
traffic noise carelessness
ceaseless speculation
affairs of opinion
cruel victimization
greed hypocrisy paradoxical ironies

So now I lay me down to sleep
not unkind
but think on Joys of Sweet Death

April Rain

April Rain
Stands firmer against thy will
Innumerable tears
Shielding uproarious fears
Contritely worn ills
Heavily they pour and soak
Leaving ecology loosened and broken

The Oak Tree stands firm
against thine will
bitter battles upon the hill
Intrinsically the waters wamble
wane swell erupt
gamble like a lottery
strange chances impart empty glares
then stares immensely against the sky

Grey dreams
Freshened colors
One voice hailed metallurgically
Systematic emphatic
New visionary prophesy

What becomes reality?
The abstinence of fantasy!

SOMEONE on the Path I Trod

Someone on the path I trod should match my quiet refrain
as I ponder reposefully the cascade stains and baleful stomps
which beat and drown my soul's disdain

Unnecessary torture resumes if underfed
presently doubtful confluences of misanthropic dread
angst annoys the state of stillness yearning
to be a more pleasing domain

Plotted near as planned more life-longed
aspirations wage yet another trial
deceivingly decisive daft how fervent
hopes and dreams do please

Did Autumn too demanding
offer callous Winter's freeze?

Floral Emergence

Spring is soon upon us
Her generous blooms assured
Reminders of renewal

We shall in faith endure
Anointed without aspersions
These visions of love pure

The GREENING Years

As the backyard becomes its own medley of
     vines and plants and flora and trees and shrubbery
The evenings feel cooler because the glow
     of colors bright and faded beckon the shift

Vines of passion, morning glory, orange trumpet
     pose the most thriving coverage yet unseen
They climb they cling they twist and hold firm
     African trees broad branches throng roots
that shape lawn folds that dip or crevice so

Seeds sown unlocked when frivolous nature
     echos the cycle of seasons reason true unknown

The Last Three Days of Summer

Three Days of Summer remain
    to heat the heart
        to warm the coolness
            of the chagrins of nature

Three Days of Summer instinctively convinced that
    Autumn will fall sudden
like the cooperative clouds of the winds

Three Days of Summer still stand to sport
    the sun mode tan
        and dark skinned style
    then back to seasoned fare
        conventional wintry ways

In Hopes of Friendship

Whittled away by shiftless dreams
And flocked with hopes of friendship
    What a beauty this unmelting iceberg
But only to touch its deceiving tip
    No change in the weather so it seems

    Counted are the many hours in passing
Each thought as with each day anew
    Shockingly the color that always strikes me
        Is cool cold blue

An ocean breeze just passed my mind
    I'm sure it must be a thought from a friend
For it was gentle refreshing and comforting strength
    Also salty-tasty was this swiftly passing wind

    Imagine the day when joy finally comes
A friendship I need, nature and Heaven, our friends indeed
    I thank you so gently and playfully
        I'll laugh and sing and dance forever

Friendship you see is a miracle in disguise
We can watch it grow with our heads to the sky

    Autumn is upon us, let's quietly gather for rest
Winter's sleep will most likely be a test
    Spring with her awakening & Summer with her heated love
Will bring about the wondrous peace of lovely flocking doves

Another hour, day has passed
    Whittled away by shiftless dreams
    In hopes of friendship

Empty Glare

Gaze beyond the horizon
and see eternal bliss
Look into a neighbor's eye
and view a world afraid

Who can answer the question
What's in store after 1984?
Children cry out in rebellion
A society, one, people on edge
slipping falling sinking
The climber's rock turns to dust
from a lack of faith and mistrust

Look into a stranger's eyes
and see a wary anger

Dear Father Help Us!
Shine your light to keep us warm
and brighten our hearts once again
Free us from the bondage of mundane sin

When we pray, please, oh please
hear our plea and show you care
look not to us with empty glare

Usurpers

Ask Ask Ask
    yet that which thou hath asked
cannot be asked of thee

Give Give Give
    that which thou hath been given
so should be given from thee

Take Take Take
    thou makest such ease of said task

Awake Awake Awake
    before 'tis too late
one must humbly surely ask

Found Doubt

Some fear I've lost optimism
    that wishful state of mind
But they're the same who cautioned me
    to view real human kind
Reality as it actually is . . .
    quit believing those corny dreams
That you can change the system
    hmmph, be happy with your genes

Well America has lied to me and worse than that
    IT Kills
The very ground it's built upon . . .
    laden avaricious wills
Too many empty promises hence 1865
    all the funky rhetoric hypocrisy and jive

Divine Potential - Is that all that we've got?
    I wonder if this is so
Because if we are without some hope
    there's nowhere left to go

Thrum Riddles

Speak thou of pennies
Speak Ye, nay, less
Quiet avaricious wantonness
Discard thine parsimonious irony

Absolute Poverty or Relative Poverty
It is - Poverty just the same

Percipient clothed naked soul
Transpires the oppressed contention
Distorted sycophant elite hypocrisy

Nay, I dare say, "Trickle - Trickle"
Weasel worded distance, but just how far?
STARVATION DAMNATION

Riddle reason ethereal, cry succinctly clear
Oh why does the afeared adversity sit here?
See sorrow shed yet another laden tear

Thrum-Riddles do answer and say
Do say and answer and answer and say
Suffering's Incompleteness

Utopian redundancy
Ignites sagacious honesty
Inspires perspicuity
Indigenous inherently
Creating curiosity
Voracious mediocrity
Computerized technology
and Universal Harmony

11 - 8 - 88

Today we know that Bush
will become our next President
and fear has gripped some hearts
What can one expect
of this new "kindler-gentler" administration
more of the same?
Times indeed are-a-changing
but when for the better? Now?

Gone are Whitman, Emerson, Thoreau and such
Now it's Stallone, Speilberg, and Capital Gain we trust

I think I shall melt away
like ice-cubes on a summer's day
become a liquid element
. . . splashing all around . . .

Funny, I forgot to say
also today, I received an awe inspiring
telephone call professing great hope
encouragement and sincerity
despite the frightful vote

Yes, Today is just as whimsical
as yesterday's hypocrisy
Surrender again, shall We?
and just await our new destiny?

Stump

The rudiments of Politics
        I cannot say 'agree'
the voice-by-proxy manner and ways
        don't seem upright to me

We watch the politicians
        in glitz and gloss, they shine
while grimy homeless families
        arrest my zealous mind

Too often I am disarrayed, for sure
        by how easily we're sold
that we shall see a "Brand New Era"
        that's fashioned on the old

What happened to the great new man
        Visionary Revolutionist
with Humanity at the Core?

Suppressed by comforts grasp
        or worse, engulfed in excess
and trapped by luxury's door
        an avaricious fantasy
                I've grown to abhor

I cannot guess nor even surmise
what's next upon the screen
a picture that repudiates
the promise of the Dream?

How much can we shoulder?
    How voluminous the demands
        before we make the change?
    Alleviate rhetoric false and unclear
Fashion a new policy admirable and sincere?

What force procures the tide?
    Centripetal no doubt
Against the haves with more and more
    AND THOSE WITH LESS WITHOUT . . .
Problematic Peace Puzzles
    Terrorizing Truth Traps and
Medicinal Media in our lives
    Do we dare address the meager crimes
of some of Today's husbands and wives?

Gorbechev Reaganomics Bush and China too?
    A deficit too high to fly
        what will politicians do?
    DESIGN A PLAN BY THE WORKERS' HAND
        to sweep our troubled land?

Unknown, as yet, we shall see . . .
  How time, this time, will unfold our destiny

Urban Plight a great dilemma
  Unresolved as if nobody's there
Who will clean the filthy seas
  and pollutants in the air?
Should we ask the Industries to limit profit gain?
Do not repeat the aforementioned or risk your thoughts insane

The graying of the U.S.A.
  is rapid and immense
so why a callous overspent campaign
  to build a brute defense?
What gives? Who takes? Why live by the rules?
Why so many buses to right the wrongs or social crisis
  invested in our schools?

Exhausting and fatiguing are the battles we must bear
  Confusing and perplexing is the lack of genuine care
  Questions are not just for asking
    They probe to find what is TRUE
      Someone great in equal faculties
      with means to do the due

Yes, who will rewrite history
and make the worthy climb
Reveal a great Democracy of integrity sublime

Care for the meek
Work for the yearning and able
Health for the families as well
Hope for the tears
Food for the starving
Nurtured wisdom for bright young minds

Is Social Justice Simply Just a Strange Desired Thing?
When on Earth
Will Victory Roar
and Sing as Wild Bells Ring?

Two Wit

This is a bid to those who care to dare
Independent of means perhaps not
An insightful scope for viewing
What we have and haven't got

Superficialities characteristic of our time
Given unto proclivities of the timid or the sublime

"This lass or that lad," said he, is as annoying as
                    any such thing that I have known."

"Despite an array or display of competencies which I esteem have
                    been consistently shown."

"Opinion more than fact or tact does weigh quite
                    heavily upon the scales."

"Misery fills the prison cells more
                    than crime does inside of our jails."

Given opportunity would with limits unclenched
                    genuine equity be our outright win inevitably?"

Or must we keep playing this game abundantly redundant
Of selective selfish senseless sorrow status stunted pundits

If I Could

I'd be an invisible molecule
    If I could I would fade
From known existence and
    Journey to a realm not
Seen by anyone not even GOD.
What's GOD to do about it anyway?

Some people are simply unkind
    Worry wand-lusting wack heads
Spreading dread in any way they choose
If I could smack good sense
    Upside their heads I would, wouldn't you?
But since I can't I won't and
Because I'm not ethereal I don't

Violence against another person (some say)
Is correctly perceived as wrong
Especially for a blocked man who
Wants to sing his song

If I could I'd set things right
I'd move 'em right along
Surer faster purer they'd be
'til injustices be gone

If I could I'd smash these
Words and grind them to a pulp
I'd be a love philanthropist
Who could never give or get enough

I just can't get enough of that
Funky stuff that soothes and grooves
That makes your mind and heart
And soul get up and bust a move

If I could I'd change the
World with a simple twist of fate
Where nothing is impossible except
Malicious cruelties rooted in vociferous hate

EYE The Fool

When poets live, their hearts may die
they seek only to love
Strange, but they may never discover why
they meet such cruelties unique
unto them
victimized incessantly
by an endearing malicious whim

Eye the fool if you will
as pithy as can be
I the fool believed in love
A love (for why) I ne'er shall see

As nature does so nature is
a give and take of sorts
bid me then this moment dry
and hear my tearful retorts

Departure

There are not many choices a poor man can make

But given too much adversity his being he will take

to the depths of purgatory and the gates of hell

to scream out with a rebel yell

He makes his departure when no one wants his arrival

Too much selective exposure - caste - class

Economy - not enough answers in Deuteronomy

Going-going-gone and the battles wager on

The man perceived as winner

is at times the greatest sinner

So an unholy option of voluntary escape doesn't seem so bad

In fact, it should leave them glad

Skeptic

I may not achieve very much you say
Yet I believe God lights my way
Earthly acclaim I might desire
Yet higher still the Lord's everlasting
Love I aspire

So go ahead and doubt what you can
Or cannot see
Yet one day you'll witness what's real for me
Liberty and justice and faith reassured
Cancer and AIDS finally cured
People laughing out of joy not spite
Sinners and saints both stand to fight
For some what is right is equally thought wrong
The elders' crass cacophony
The youngers' euphonious song

Tonight and the morning
The day and the eve

Destination contemplations
Situations we must leave

Uncertainties abundantly availed
Opinions of decisions of visionaries impaled
Refused equal access to riches
Henceforth untold

Accepting not expecting these
Stories we are sold

Why risk a badge of complacency?
Instead be brash be bold

Truth is in the pudding,
but laminated lies are just plain old

Brothers Bring It

Everybody thinks they know me
But honestly they don't

They could stop all the gossip and get it right
But they won't

So let me set the record straight
And make it absolutely clear

Yo (stuff/shit) is based on garbage
And yo motivation's fear

Yo mama must be stupid
And yo daddy must be dumb
Cuz when I hit you with the
Cold hard truth you'll be feeling lost and numb

(I'll) have you crying like a baby
And screaming like a bitch
Make you wanna change ya plans
Have you scratchin' that itch

You can scandalize my name
Try to vilify the truth
But nothin' from nothin' ain't nothin'
(fool) withouth proof

So 'fess up homey; come correct
Wuz the deal?
Stop frontin'/ quit bull (shhhh…)
Straight up [vato] just be real

I hate to break it to you
And say "I told you so!"
But you ain't nothin' but a skeezah
Peace out, I gots tah go…
Hold up—bet you thought I was gone
Yeah you can keep it comin'
If you want a sho' nuff hood hard battle… it's on

Nah—ain't no use for violence
You don't need to get a gun 'cause
No matter what you shoot at me
I'll still be number one
Now we can come together
We can surely work it out <yup>
Unity, community is
What it's all about

Disposable

Americans love to toss their trash
And celebrate their excess and waste

Seems it hasn't any worth if it doesn't
Take cash - commendable collateral a sound fiscal savings capital
Patience be gone, we'd rather just do it in haste

Goals or Dreams
< passion filled / packages of / hopeful aspirations >
We'll vociferously smash - -
Money's misinformation lasts but does not compute
And the truth? Hah, better learn how to lie,
Just in case {what you may face} *
A chance or circumstance that leaves you disgraced
Because you're virtually disposable in this God forsaken place

An Anorectic Agent

Anomy an enemy
  Zeitgeist perverse untoward
Cruel fate awaits the desperate cries
  Of those deferred inequitably selected
Rejected unprotected or worse insulted
Even when one has given one's best efforts thwarted
  Postponed ceased menially shown unknown
Ethereal unseen no reason real brought forth
Malevolence unchallenged wildly untamed

So it should not be as shocking as such
A gruesome gasp blankly born from fright
For in those times of calculated tyranny
  What's wrong with being right?
Too many calling shots care not for
What they do hurt deceive believe
The worst not truth whilst throngs sit
Lamenting because they cannot too weak
  Freely speak dare stand bare-boned
Starved and despondent we leave be
To act alone abandoned isolated cold

Thirsty their unquenched hunger unfulfilled
Why not feed our best impulses to do good works
Well done more or less we cry whilst
Shown saddened shadows as we shift
Or perish in gutless garb unfitting nor apt it
Dangles off hangers of our soulless selves
Too thin to hold dreams and hopes
We once dared reverently bold perchance to make
Untold scolded suspect and queried about
Hearts hurt moreover hardened and souled out
Please survey these warning signs
Lest we be kept without

Better Blurred

Sometimes I remove my glasses
To see things less corrected [to shift]

The right perspective to be more suitably

Connected

Blurry unfocused I cannot
See you as you might portentously be

But my gaze upon what is
Unclear becomes endearing
Because I might not see you as
You are in others' sight
But what I see is you
As flawed as me maybe
Misunderstood uncool old-fashioned
But true

Abash Virility

Loosened vile thoughts
    Actions worse abstained
        pleasing pornographic
            abeyance

    Rebel victory
        causes no alarm
    Meeting raptured loins
        Destined desires
    Moist and sticky
        Hard and hot indulgence
Stimuli apparent

        Denial forged
    Requisition indignity
    Pushed fondled spoiled

Erectus magnanimous - convergence

Seekers

WE SEEK NOT OF YOUR VISION

WE SEEK NOT THE VISION OF SIGHT

ORDAINED, BE BLINDED BY COMPASSION'S WAVE

INDIFFERENT TO YOUR PLIGHT

WE SANCTIFY THE REVERENT

NEBULOUSLY, WE ADMONISH NEW HEIGHTS

Harbinger

Flash   Flash   Flash
    Tip-Toe   Tattle-tale
Sneak up   a-front-a-ya

Nothing hidden
    unless you're looking
Premonition secrecy
    Another theme dream
Old Indian saves lives
    lifts souls and goals
Stooping won't raise you
    reaching will shake your fall

    What's Up Ahead?
Can you see what you know must be?
    Are You, Have You, Will You?

Man Aphotic

Heretic Prophesy
cancels the storm
Omnipotent fingertips revenge malady

Stand Man Aphotic
and then sit thee down
Herald New Age One
Share Life's Gift Humanity
Rest Now Brotherhood

We camp the fire is warm
the cold hardened habit
to beckon what belies
beyond the finite hour
prism spectrum sights
Aphrodite entice crimson candles
jaded soldier surrender
Imaginative Enthusiast
Expressions of Life Love Joy Peace Freedom
Emotions that Teach the Spirit to Fly
As the audience confers its querry
Balance Control Purpose
Man Aphotic and Soon We Prosper

Balance

A Fractal Fantasy

Quantum Relativity Space Time Gravity
Tiny Small Mighty Expansive Vast Big

Einstein Oppenheimer & Other Expeditious Physicists
Master Designers of Nuclear Energy & the Atomic Bomb
Volatile Revelations of What's Right & What's Wrong

Scholars and Scientists Have Been Soundly Advised
An Evolution Revolution Which Cannot Be Televised
Our Past Hopes Diminished Anticipation Vaporized

Electrons Quarks Quasars Cosmology Beyond Our Scope
Big Bang Theory Black Holes & All That We Suppose
$E=mc^2$ Was Most Certainly An All Time Explosive Hit
A Calculated Scientific Fit You Simply Must Admit

Unified Field Theory Best Known As One That Failed
A New World Order Technologically Advanced Derailed

If We Glance Into the Future Shall We See Life Enhanced
All That We Are Or All That We Can Be As One Advanced

Problems Never Go Away We Just Have More of the Same
If We Do Not Fix How Aliens Ail Us Just Who Is To Blame

Answer We

The Riddle of the Sphinx cannot be solved
          no matter how man's great evolutionary science
or our advanced modern technology is involved
          to our collective dismay it ever yet stands tall

3000 years it has formidably withstood men
          of tyrannical intent caged by cycles of war
or liberated during causes of humanitarian good

Canon blasts upon its nose
          exploded at the base of its loins
scavenged its treasured mysteries
          and has greedily stolen its gold coins

Even to the very top of the Ancient Pyramids of Egypt
          we might climb
what lies beyond its apex mankind may never find

We seek in great endeavor yet our quest remains
          unfulfilled perhaps because the wills of man
are so easily eclipsed by our selfish disequilibrium
          our obviously inept discovery skills

Dawns of ages have come and gone
          yet the problematic quandaries we face
remain inane
          so what's really going on?

Answer me
Answer we
Answer us
Answer them

Is the Riddle of the Sphinx our reminder to condemn
        all that is blasphemous malevolent untrue
or is the Sphinx's Riddle merely a simple question that
        we must face as one time tested forever true too?

Look into its eyes as we might gaze into the looking glass
        the wind swept shifting sands of time
ever changing occasionally pass swiftly as it asks
        quietly defiantly passionately

WHO ARE YOU?

CPSIA information can be obtained at www.ICGtesting.com
Printed in the USA
LVOW06s2159310713

345718LV00001B/13/P